THE LITTLE BOOK OF !#!?
BOOK OF
FOREIGN
SWEAR
WORDS

THE LITTLE BOOK OF FOREIGN SWEAR WORDS

This edition copyright © Summersdale Publishers Ltd, 2015

First published in 2012 as *Essential Foreign Swear Words*

Summersdale Publishers Ltd
46 West Street
Chichester
West Sussex
PO19 1RP
UK

www.summersdale.com

Printed and bound in Malta

ISBN: 978-1-84953-771-1

Substantial discounts on bulk quantities of Summersdale books are available to corporations, professional associations and other organisations. For details contact general enquiries: telephone: +44 (0) 1243 771107 or email: enquiries@summersdale.com.

THE LITTLE BOOK OF !#!?

FOREIGN SWEAR WORDS

Sid Finch

summersdale

Disclaimer

Summersdale Publishers cannot be held responsible for any uncomfortable, unfriendly or unusual situations arising from the misuse of this book.

CONTENTS

Note

These translations are correct to the best of our knowledge. If you have an alternative suggestion for any of our translations, please let us know!

INTRODUCTION

When you go on holiday abroad, it's important to be able to communicate with the natives. It's useful to know, for example, whether the policeman who is trying to bundle you into the back of a van is calling you a bastard or a cunt. Or, perhaps your plateful of foreign nosh has a distinctly faecal aroma and you want to make sure the waiter understands what you're shouting about. With this book, not only will you be able to translate the abuse being thrown at you, you will also be able to dish it out in dirty great spades. Happy swearing!

SWEAR WORDS

ARSE

French *Cul*

German *Arsch*

Italian *Culo*

Spanish *Culo*

ARSEHOLE

French *Trou de cul*

German *Arschloch*

Italian *Stronzo*

Spanish *Gilipollas*

ARSEWIPE

French *Papier cul*

German *Scheisshauspapier*

Italian *Leccaculo*

Spanish *Culo limpie*

BALL-SUCKER

French *Lécheur de couilles*

German *Eierlutscher*

Italian *Succhia palle*

Spanish *Lechón testículo*

BALLS

French *Couilles*

German *Eier*

Italian *Palle*

Spanish *Huevos*

BASTARD

French *Fils de pute*

German *Hurensohn*

Italian *Bastardo*

Spanish *Cabrón*

BITCH

French *Salope*

German *Schlampe*

Italian *Puttana*

Spanish *Zorra*

BLOODY HELL!

French *Putain!*

German *Verdammte Scheisse!*

Italian *Maledizione!*

Spanish *¡Coño!*

BLOW JOB

French *Pipe*

German *Dick Blasen*

Italian *Pompino*

Spanish *Mamada*

BOLLOCKS

French *Conneries*

German *Eier*

Italian *Coglioni*

Spanish *Cojones*

BUGGER IT!

French *Merde alors!*

German *Scheiss drauf!*

Italian *Fanculo!*

Spanish *¡Me cago en la puta!*

BULLSHIT

French *Conneries*

German *Kacke*

Italian *Stronzata*

Spanish *Mierda de toro*

CAMEL TOE

French *Doigt de pied de chameau*

German *Sich abzeichnende Schamlippen*

Italian *Zoccolo d' cammello*

Spanish *Camello dedo del pie*

CHOAD

French *Pénis court graisse*

German *Würfelschwanz*

Italian *Salsicciotto*

Spanish *Pene pequísimo*

COCK

French *Bite*

German *Schwanz*

Italian *Cazzo*

Spanish *Polla*

COCK-SUCKER

French *Lécheur de boule*

German *Schwanzlecker*

Italian *Ciuccia cazzo*

Spanish *Chupa pollas*

CUNT

French *Salaud*

German *Fotze*

Italian *Figa*

Spanish *Coño*

DAMN!

French *Merde!*

German *Verdammt!*

Italian *Maledizione!*

Spanish *¡Caray!*

DICK

French *Bitte*

German *Schwanz*

Italian *Cazzo*

Spanish *Polla*

DICKHEAD

French *Tête de bite*

German *Schwanzkopf*

Italian *Testa di cazzo*

Spanish *Gilipollas*

DILDO

French *Godemichet*

German *Dildo*

Italian *Dildo*

Spanish *Consolador*

DOUCHEBAG

French *Crétin*

German *Intimdusche*

Italian *Cretino*

Spanish *Gilipollas*

DUMB ARSE

French *Débil*

German *Dummkopf*

Italian *Idiota*

Spanish *Idiota*

French *Pet*

German *Furz*

Italian *Scoreggia*

Spanish *Pedo*

FUCK

French *Baiser*

German *Ficken*

Italian *Scopare*

Spanish *Joder*

FUCK FACE

French *Face de pet*

German *Fickgesicht*

Italian *Faccia da cazzo*

Spanish *Gilipollas*

FUR-BURGER

French *Hamburger de fourrure*

German *Fellburger*

Italian *Hamburger peloso*

Spanish *Conejo*

GASH

French *Balafre*

German *Fotze*

Italian *Figa*

Spanish *Brecha*

GOAT-FUCKER

French *Niquer de chèvres*

German *Ziegeficker*

Italian *Trombatore di capre*

Spanish *Hijo de cabra*

HOLY SHIT!

French *Bordel de merde!*

German *Heilige Scheisse!*

Italian *Porca merda!*

Spanish *¡Mierda santo!*

MERKIN

French *Perruque pubienne*

German *Schamhaartoupet*

Italian *Pelo pubico*

Spanish *Peluca púbico*

MOTHERFUCKER

French *Tu niques ta mere*

German *Mutterficker*

Italian *Figlio di puttana*

Spanish *Hijo de puta*

MUFF-DIVING

French *Lécher une foufoune*

German *Muschitauchen*

Italian *Mangiara figa*

Spanish *Buceo mata*

PISS

French *Pisse*

German *Pisse*

Italian *Piscio*

Spanish *Meada*

PUSSY

French *Chatte*

German *Muschi*

Italian *Bagiana*

Spanish *Panocha*

SHIT

French *Merde*

German *Scheisse*

Italian *Merda*

Spanish *Mierda*

SON OF A BITCH

French *Fils de pute*

German *Hurensohn*

Italian *Figlio di puttana*

Spanish *Hijo de puta*

TITS

French *Nichons*

German *Titten*

Italian *Tette*

Spanish *Tetas*

WANKER

French *Branleur*

German *Wichser*

Italian *Segaiolo*

Spanish *Pajero*

WHORE

French *Putain*

German *Hure*

Italian *Troia*

Spanish *Puta*

WILLY

French *Zizi*

German *Schniedel*

Italian *Pistolino*

Spanish *Colita*

SHORT
SWEAR
PHRASES

FUCK OFF!

French *Va te faire foutre!*

German *Verpiss dich!*

Italian *Vaffanculo!*

Spanish *¡Vete a tomar por culo!*

PAIN IN THE ARSE

French *Emmerdeur*

German *Saumässig nervig*

Italian *Rompicoglioni*

Spanish *Que coño*

SHIT FOR BRAINS

....

French *Cerveau de merde*

German *Kackbratze*

Italian *Testa di cazzo*

Spanish *Tu cerebro esta hecho de mierda*

KISS MY ARSE!

French *Touche mon cul!*

German *Leck mich am Arsch!*

Italian *Leccami il culo!*

Spanish *¡Puedes besar mi culo!*

YOU STINK OF SHIT

French *Tu pues comme la merde*

German *Du stinkst nach Scheisse*

Italian *Puzzi di merda*

Spanish *Apestas a mierda*

ROPEY OLD SLAG

French *Vieille pute visqueuse*

German *Verseuchte alte Nutte*

Italian *Vecchia bagascia schifosa*

Spanish *Vieja puta*

YOU FAT BASTARD!

French *Gros bâtard!*

German *Du fette Sau!*

Italian *Grasso bastardo!*

Spanish *¡Gordo cabrón!*

SHOVE IT UP YOUR ARSE!

French *Enfonce-le-toi dans le cul!*

German *Steckst dir im Hintern!*

Italian *Mettitelo nel culo!*

Spanish *¡Saca eso de tu culo!*

UGLY FUCKER

French *Sale enculé*

German *Hässliches Arschloch*

Italian *Brutto stronzo*

Spanish *Guarro*

French *Pauvre crétin!*

German *Du unnötiges Unwesen!*

Italian *Inetto imbecille!*

Spanish *¡Eres muy puta!*

EAT SHIT
AND DIE!

French *Mange de la merde et meurs!*

German *Friss Scheisse und stirb!*

Italian *Mangia merda e crepa!*

Spanish *¡Come mierda y muerte!*

YOU FREAK!

French *Monstre!*

German *Du Freak!*

Italian *Scherzo della natura!*

Spanish *¡Tu raro!*

YOU WERE HIT WITH THE UGLY STICK

French *Tu t'es fait toucher avec le baton des moches*

German *Du wurdest mit dem hässlichen Stock geschlagen*

Italian *Siete stati colpiti con il brutto bastone*

Spanish *Usted fue golpeado con el palo feo*

YOUR FACE LOOKS LIKE A BALLSACK

French *Tête de coquilles*

German *Du Sackgesicht*

Italian *La tua faccia sembra un sacco da pucile*

Spanish *Su cara se parece a los testículos*

SILLY BITCH!

French *Stupide putain!*

German *Dumme Schlampe!*

Italian *Stupida puttana!*

Spanish *¡Perra tonta!*

GO FUCK YOURSELF!

French *Va te faire enculer!*

German *Fick dich!*

Italian *Vaffanculo!*

Spanish *¡Vete a la mierda!*

!#!?

LONG
SWEAR
PHRASES

Your country is like a toilet. It doesn't need a president; it just needs someone to flush all the shit away.

French

Votre pays se ressemble une toilette. Il n'a pas besoin d'un président, il a besoin de quelqu'un pour vider toute la merde.

German

Dein Land is wie ein Klo. Ihr braucht keinen Präsidenten, sondern nür einen, der die Scheisse wegspült.

Italian

Il vostro paese è come un gabinetto. Non ha bisogno di un presidente, ma di qualcuno che tiri giu' l'acqua per far sparire tutta la merda.

Spanish

Tu país es como un wáter. No necesita un presidente sino alguien que tire de la cadena para que se vaya la mierda.

Can you drink the water here, or does it taste of piss, like your beer?

French
L'eau ici est-elle potable, ou a-t-elle le goût de pisse, comme votre bière?

German
Kann man das Wasser hier trinken, oder schmeckt es auch nach Pisse wie euer Bier?

Italian
Potete bere l'acqua qui, o sa di piscia come la vostra birra?

Spanish
¿Se puede beber el agua aquí o sabe a pis como vuestra cerveza?

I would rather fuck a donkey than you.

French
J'aimerais mieux foutre un âne que toi.

German
Ich werde ehe ein Esel ficken wie du.

Italian
Preferire scopare con un asino che te.

Spanish
Prefiero follar un burro que follar a ti.

You have the charm of a pair of shitty underpants.

French
T'es aussi charmant qu'un slip merdique.

German
Du bist so charmant wie beschissene Unterwäsche.

Italian
Hai il fascino di un paio di mutande sporche di merda.

Spanish
Tienes el encanto como calzoncillos llena de mierda.

I wouldn't touch you with a shitty stick.

French
*Je ne te toucherais pas même
avec un bâton merdique.*

German
*Ich würde dich nicht mal mit 'nem
beschissenen Besenstiel berühren.*

Italian
*Non ti toccherei con un
bastone coperto merda.*

Spanish
No te tocaría ni con un palo lleno de mierda.

Put a toilet on your head and keep it there while I shit on you.

French
Mets toi une cuvette sur la tête pour que j'y chie.

German
Setz dir eine Toilette auf den Kopf und halt sie fest bis ich fertig geschissen habe.

Italian
Mettiti un cesso in testa cosi' cago su di te.

Spanish
Ponte un retrete en la cabeza y aguántalo mientras yo me cago en ti.

You smell like a monkey's arse.

French
Tu pues comme un cul de singe.

German
Du riechst wie ein Affenarsch.

Italian
Puzzi come il culo di una scimmia.

Spanish
Hueles como el culo de un mono.

Your football team is shit.

French
Ton équipe de foot est de la merde.

German
Dein Verein ist Scheisse.

Italian
La vostra squadra di calcio e'una merda.

Spanish
Tu equipo de fútbol es una puta mierda.

Your penis is so small that a mouse wouldn't notice if you fucked it.

French
Ta pine est si petite que si tu baisais une souris elle ne le remarquerais pas.

German
Dein Schwanz ist so klein, dass es 'ne Maus nicht merkt, wenn du sie fickst.

Italian
Hai un pene così piccolo che se scopi un topo non se ne accorge nemmeno.

Spanish
Tu pene es tan pequeño que si te follaras a un ratón, no lo notaría.

Your country is shit.
Your food is shit.
Your beer is shit.
I could go on...

French
Votre pays est merde. Votre nourriture est merde. Votre bière est merde. Je peux continuer...

German
Euer Land ist Scheisse. Euer Essen ist Scheisse. Euer Bier ist Scheisse. So könnte ich weitermachen...

Italian
Il tuo e' un paese di merda. Con cibo di merda. Birra di merda. E potrei continuare cosi'...

Spanish
Tu país es una mierda. Vuestra comida una mierda. Vuestra cerveza una mierda. Podría seguir...

Are you in training for the 'Slag of the Year' contest?

French
Peut-être que tu t'entraînes pour devenir 'Pute de l'Année'?

German
Trainierst du schon für die 'Schlampe des Jahres' wettbewerb?

Italian
Ti stai allenando per diventare la 'Puttana dell'Anno'?

Spanish
¿Entrenas para el concurso de la 'Zorra del Año'?

I wouldn't piss on you if you were on fire.

French
Je ne pisserais pas au-dessus de toi meme si tu étais en feu.

German
Ich würde nicht mal auf dich pissen, wenn du brennst.

Italian
Non piscerei su di te se fosti in fiamme.

Spanish
No te meo aun si estabas en llamas.

Excuse me, waiter, you silly bastard. I ordered chips.

French
Excusez-moi, garcon, con débile.
J'ai commandé des frites.

German
Entschuldigung, Herr Ober, idiotischer
Mistkerl, ich habe Pommes bestellt.

Italian
Scusi, cameriere, cretino bastardo.
Ho ordinato delle patatine fritte.

Spanish
Perdón, camarero, tu gilipollas.
He pedido patatas fritas.

Did you spill my drink, you fuckwit?

French
Tu as renversé mon biosson, crétin?

German
Hast du meinen schnapps verschüttet, Volltrottel?

Italian
Hai rovesciato il mio bevanda, testa di cazzo?

Spanish
¿Me has tirado la bebida, tu cabrón?

This beach is taken, so piss off.

French
Cette plage est réservée, alors casse-toi.

German
Dieser Strand ist reserviert, also verpiss dich.

Italian
Questa spiaggia è riservata, vaffanculo.

Spanish
Esta playa es reservada, vete a la mierda.

That's pissed me off!

French
Ça me fait chier!

German
Das kotzt mir an!

Italian
Questo mi fa' incazzare!

Spanish
¡Que me cabreo!

I have you down as a bit of a pigeon-licker.

French
Je t'ai pris comme un lècheur de pigeons.

German
Ich wette du bist ein Taubenlecker.

Italian
Ti facevo come un lecca piccioni nel tuo tempo libero.

Spanish
Tengo que bajar como alguien que lame palomas.

Where I come from, fucking your siblings is not encouraged.

French
A mon pays, l'incest n'est pas encouragé.

German
Da wo ich herkomme, wird Sex mit seinem Geschwistern nicht gefördert.

Italian
Nel mio paese l'incesto non e' incoraggiato.

Spanish
De dónde yo vengo, el incesto no esta bien visto.

Is that a suntan or do you have shit on your fingers?

French
Tu t'est bronzé ou tu as de la merde sur les doigts?

German
Hast du Sonnenbrand oder hast du Scheisse an den Fingern?

Italian
Sei abbronzato o hai della merda sulle dita?

Spanish
¿Eso es moreno o es que tienes mierda en los dedos?

You're as ugly as an old potato.

French
Tu es aussi moche qu'une vielle patate.

German
Du bist hässlich wie eine alte Kartoffel.

Italian
Sei brutto come una vecchia potato.

Spanish
Usted es tan feo como una patata vieja.

RANDOM SWEAR WORDS FROM AROUND THE WORLD

Afrikaans

Fuck you: *Fok jou*

Cunt: *Poes*

You cunt: *Jou poes*

Wank: *Trek draad*

Put your head inside a cow's front bottom and wait for a bull to take you up the arse: *Sit jou kop in die koei se kont en wag tot die bul jou kom holnaai*

Arabic

Tits: *Biz*

Kiss my arse: *Boos teezee*

Shit: *Chraa*

Shit on you: *Charra alaik*

Fuck you: *Cus*

Bastard: *Sharmute*

Knob: *Zib*

Fuck me: *Nek ni*

Shut up: *Kul khara*

Chinese (Cantonese)

I need a shit: *Ah si*

Cunt: *Hai*

Whore: *Gai*

Eat shit: *Sek si*

Fuck: *D'iu*

Fuck your mother's front botty:
D'iu nei lo mo hai

Chinese (Mandarin)

Cunt: *Bi*

Bastard: *Liu mang*

Fuck your mother: *Gan ni lao ma*

Shit: *Ta ma de*

Big tits: *Bo ba*

Knob: *Diao*

Fuck off: *Gun dan*

Dutch

To fart: *Broekhoesten*

Cunt: *Flamoes*

Fuck: *Een wip maken*

Knob: *Lul*

Sperm: *Kwakkie*

Motherfucker: *Moederneuker*

Testical-washer: *Zakkewasser*

Arse: *Reet*

Bastard: *Schoft*

! # ! ?

Esperanto

Arsehole: *Anusulo*

Shit: *Fek*

Fuck: *Fiki*

To fart: *Furzi*

To shit: *Kaki*

Knob: *Kako*

Arse: *Pugo*

Motherfucker: *Patrinfi kulo*

To bugger: *Bugri*

To give a blow job: *Midzi*

French

You're pissing me off:
Tu m'emmerdes

Eat shit: *Va bouffer ta merde*

Go tinker with yourself:
Va te tripoter

Droopy tits: *Bloblos*

Poo: *Caca*

Piss: *Pisse*

Enormously capacious knockers:
Il y a du monde au balcon

Hair pie: *Foufoune*

You bastard! I'll smash your face in:
*Espece de salaud! Je vais vous
casser la gueule*

I want to punch someone:
*Je voudrais donner un coup de
poing à quelqu'un*

German

Fuck me: *Fick mich*

Slut: *Schlampe*

To ejaculate: *Abspritzen*

Cunt juice: *Moesensaft*

Tits: *Titten*

To vomit: *Reihern*

Someone who shits their pants:
Hosenscheisser

To give a blow job: *Jemandem
einen blasen*

Male prostitute: *Stricher*

Greek

Wanker: *Malakas*

Someone who has fun with his arse: *Pisoglentis*

Back-door sex: *Pisokolito*

Shit: *Skata*

Bullshit: *Hyessou*

Go fuck a cow: *Lech zayen para*

Lick my arse: *Lakek et hatahat sheli*

Penis: *Zayin*

Son of a bitch: *Ben zsona*

To hell with your fucking father:
Inahl rabak ars ya choosharmuta

Italian

I don't give a shit: *No me ne frega un cazzo*

Piece of shit: *Pezzo di merda*

Fuck your mother: *Scopa tua mamma*

To come in your pants: *Venire nei pantaloni*

Suck my knob: *Succhiami il cazzo*

Sheep-shagging: *Pecorina*

Tit-wank: *Spagnola*

To deflower a virgin: *Sverginare*

That girl has a hot cunt: *Quella ragazza ha la figa bollente*

Arse-licker: *Leccaculo*

Japanese

Stupid: *Baka*

Arsehole: *Bakayarou*

Dickhead: *Chipatama*

Old fart: *Kusojiji*

Die shitting: *Kuso shite shinezo*

Portuguese

I'm having an orgasm: *Eu estou gozando*

Clitoris: *Grelo*

Fuck it: *Foda-se*

Fuck you: *Vai-te foder*

Russian

Oh shit, bitch: *Bl'ad*

Bastard: *Govn'uk*

To fuck: *Ebat'*

Suck my cock: *Kurite moju trubku*

Cunt: *Pizda*

Fuck off: *Yeb vas*

Tits: *Siski*

Fuck you: *Ëb tvoju mat'*

Serbian

Drop dead, redneck ox:
Crko dabogda stoko seljacka

Twat: *Govedo*

I fuck your sunshine: *Jebem ti sunce*

Eat shit: *Jedi govno*

Cock: *Kurac*

Cunt: *Picka*

Testicles: *Jaje*

Spanish

I shit in your milk: *Me cago en la leche*

Motherfucker: *Hijo de puta*

Shove a stick up your arse: *Metete un palo en el culo*

To take it up the arse: *Dar candela por el culo*

To lick a front bottom: *Hacer la sopa*

To swing both ways: *Jugar a los dos bandos*

To do it doggy-style: *Posición de mira quien viene*

Saggy tits: *Los mangos bajitos*

Your mother has a knob: *Tu madre tiene pene*

Burglar who shits on the floor: *Zorrero*

THE LITTLE
BOOK OF
DIRTY
JOKES

Sid Finch

THE LITTLE BOOK OF DIRTY JOKES

Sid Finch

£5.99
Paperback
ISBN: 978-1-84953-785-8

What do you call a cheap circumcision?

A rip-off!

Filled with more filth than three-week-old underwear, this little collection of obscene one-liners, smutty shenanigans and graphic gags will have you blushing like a freshly spanked bottom and sniggering like a naughty schoolkid.

If you're interested in finding out more about our books, find us on Facebook at **Summersdale Publishers** and follow us on Twitter at **@Summersdale**.

www.summersdale.com